THE AUTHOR

Martin Bagness is known to many mount. setter and co-organiser of the Rohan Rock ᴀ the Saunders Lakeland Mountain Marathon. He has been a member of the British O competing in six world championships with ᴀ ᴠᴇᴇᴛ ᴘᴌᴀᴄᴵᴺᴦ ᴏᵢ 16th. Since 1984 he has held the position of Coach to the British U21 Orienteering Team.

Martin is himself an enthusiastic competitor in fell races and mountain marathons. He lives in Ambleside and likes nothing better than to "get out on the fells".

FOREWORD

This book should be required reading for all fell runners and mountain marathoners. Martin tackles every aspect of mountain navigation in a straightforward and comprehensive style. He has made a major contribution to the safety of mountain runners.

Selwyn Wright, Chairman of the Fell Runners Association

CONTENTS

1   The Map 6

2   Using A Map; The Basics 11

3   Copying Down A Course 12

4   The Compass 15

5   Distance Estimation 20

6   Route Choice 22

7   Route Choice For Score Classes 29

8   Rough Navigation 32

9   Fine Navigation 34

10 Understanding Contours 39

11 Relocation 41

12 Training For Improvement 44

13 Navigating In "Traditional" Fell Races 46

14 Some Common Mistakes 50

15 Safety 52

16 The Good Race Guide 53

INTRODUCTION

This book is written for competitors in fell races and mountain marathons, and for anyone who enjoys making lightweight trips into the mountains armed with a map, compass and running shoes.

The British fell racing calender is crammed with a variety of events, with winning times varying between ten minutes and five hours. Many of the longer races require the use of some navigation skills, and even if the route is well-known beforehand, and there are other runners around, things can get very much harder when the mist comes down and the field becomes scattered. Everyone must have come to grief at some time, even the best amongst us, as is illustrated by a recent British Champion who was leading the Langdale race and emerged from the clouds at Wrynose Pass when he was looking for the Pike of Blisco!

Mountain Marathons have grown steadily in popularity since the first Karrimor was held in 1968. Far from being an offshoot of fell running or orienteering, mountain marathons are now firmly established as a sport in their own right. For a huge following of enthusiasts, mountain marathons represent the highlight of the running season. It is easy to become hooked on the pleasures and even some of the pains of mountain marathons: the feeling of excitement when preparing in the chill first light on Saturday morning; the hushed atmosphere of a midway camp lit by the glow of a hundred head torches; the taste of that first plastic cup of soup at the finish! Everyone, from beginner to expert, can improve their results by improving their navigation, but skillful navigation can be enjoyable in itself. Read this book, and hopefully the thrill of successful navigation will be added to all the other pleasures of running on the fells and moors and in the mountains.

USING THIS HANDBOOK

The techniques described in this handbook have been taken from a variety of sources. Some have arisen from the author's own experiences, whilst some have been gleaned from conversations with other enthusiastic fell runners and mountain marathoners. Others have been "borrowed" from the sport of orienteering.

The first chapters are written with the beginner in mind, however they contain a number of hints that may be new even to the expert. It is not necessary to use every method of navigation described here, instead it is better to pick and choose between the various techniques, with the aim of developing a personal "style" of navigation most suited to yourself and to the kind of races you take part in.

Navigation is a practical skill. As such you can only learn so much about it from a book. The only way to really improve your navigation is to go out running and practise the techniques described here, either during a training session or in a race.

1   THE MAP

Maps are the tools of the trade! This chapter describes those maps most commonly used in British fell races and mountain marathons: Ordnance Survey (or OS) maps at scales of 1:50000 and 1:25000, and Harvey maps at 1:40000. Apart from having different scales, these maps also use different symbols and use a different style of mapping to show the ground. Each of them has its advantages and disadvantages for the runner. A colour section from each of these maps is printed on the back cover of this handbook.

MAP SYMBOLS

	OS 1:50 000	OS 1:25000	HARVEYS 1:40 000	
road				**BLACK SYMBOLS**
track or forest - road	======	======	— — — —	
footpath	— — — —	....	— — — —	
intermittent footpath	not shown	not shown	— — — —	
railway				
buildings	□ ⌐⌐ (pink infill)	▫ ⌐⌐ (pink infill)	▪■▪	
ruin or sheepfold	not shown	□ ◠	□ ᴄ ᴇ	
trig. point	△	△	△	
boundary wall or fence	not shown			
ruined boundary	not shown	not shown		
scree				
loose rock / boulders	not shown			
large single boulder	not shown	not shown	.	
large cairn	not shown	not shown	▲	
large crag	(downslope ↓)			
outcrop			not shown	
footbridge	||	|| FB	||	
lake	◌	◌	◌	**BLUE**
river	∼∼∼	∼∼∼	∼∼∼	
wide stream				
stream				
marsh	not shown			
peat hags	not shown	not shown	ᐱᐱᐱ	
coniferous forest	🌲 🌲	🌲 🌲		**GREEN**
deciduous forest	🍃 🍃	🍃 🍃		
dense forest	not shown	not shown	dark green	
firebreak	not shown	======		
improved pasture	not shown	not shown	bright yellow	**YELLOW**
rough pasture	not shown	not shown	pale yellow	
public footpath	— — — (red)	— — — (green)	.... (green)	**PUBLIC RIGHTS OF WAY**
public bridleway	— — — (red)	— — — (green)	▫ ▫ ▫ ▫ (green)	
public telephone	☎ (black)	☎ (blue)	☎ (green)	**SAFETY**
mountain rescue kit	not shown	MOUNTAIN RESCUE KIT → (red)	⊕ (green)	

ORDNANCE SURVEY 1:50000

The most recent 1:50000 series is called the "Landranger" and covers the whole of Scotland, Wales and England in 204 sheets. The OS Mountain Trial race always uses the Landranger series. The Rohan Rock and Run Mountain Marathon sometimes uses it together with OS maps at a scale of 1:25000.

SCALE:
2 centimetres on the map equal 1 kilometre on the ground.
(Or, if you prefer, 1.25 inches equals 1 mile). As on the other maps described here, grid lines are exactly 1 kilometre apart.

CONTOUR INTERVAL:
Contours are at a vertical interval of 10 metres, with Index Contours, (the thicker lines) at 50 metres. On older 1:50000 maps contours may be at 15 metres. These are based on the old 50 foot contours and are much less accurate.

ADVANTAGES:
- Gives a good, clear picture of the overall shape of the ground, especially the patterns of the major hills and valleys.
- Each sheet covers a large area, so it is good value for money!
- Familiar to many long-time users of the fells.

DISADVANTAGES:
- In order to show a large area of ground on a small area of paper, a great deal of fine detail has been omitted. This makes it difficult to navigate to a small feature, and in fact the 1:50000 scale on its own is unsuitable for competitions involving fine navigation.

MAP HINTS:
- Fences and walls are only shown where they follow a forest boundary.
- Only the largest paths and streams are shown.
- Marshy ground is never shown in the mountains.
- Rocky ground is only sometimes shown.
- Crags are either shown as outcrops or as cliffs; outcrops are too vaguely shown to help with navigation, whereas cliffs tend to be large and obvious.
- The use of 10 metre contours at this scale means that sections of contour line are often omitted for clarity on very steep slopes.

ORDNANCE SURVEY 1:25000

The whole of Scotland, Wales and England are covered by the "Pathfinder" series (green covers). National Parks and other scenic areas are covered by the "Outdoor Leisure" series (yellow covers) or by the "Mountainmaster" series. All the major mountain marathons are occasionally held on 1:25000 maps.

SCALE:

4 centimetres on the map equal 1 kilometre on the ground.
(Or 2.5 inches equal 1 mile).

CONTOUR INVERVAL:

Contours are at a vertical interval of 10 metres, with Index Contours at 50 metres.

ADVANTAGES:

- A great deal of detail can be shown at 1:25000, making it possible to map read very accurately.

DISADVANTAGES:

- The contour lines are finely drawn, making them difficult to see during a race.
- A clutter of symbols showing different types of rocky ground and vegetation obscure the contours and make it hard to gain an overall picture of the shape of the ground.
- Pathfinder sheets cover too small an area for most races, whereas Outdoor Leisure sheets are too large and awkward to fold!

MAP HINTS:

- All walls and fences are shown. Sheepfolds are shown.
- The smallest streams, ponds and footpaths are shown, however these are not always reliable.
- As a rough guide, streams shown with a double line are uncrossable when in flood. This can be useful in Scotland where a wee spot of rain can turn the smallest burns into raging torrents! The contours on recent series have been replotted and are generally reliable.
- County and Constituency boundaries could possibly be mistaken for footpaths, although they are drawn with a much heavier line.

The "Harvey Mountain Map" series covers selected mountain areas through-out Great Britain. Used for the Saunders Lakeland Mountain Marathon, the Rohan Rock and Run Mountain Marathon and the Karrimor International Mountain Marathon. A new map is produced for each Karrimor.

SCALE:
2.5 centimetres on the map equals 1 kilometre on the ground.
(Or 1.5 inches equal 1 mile).

CONTOUR INTERVAL:
Contours are at a vertical interval of 15 metres, with Index Contours at 75 metres. Extra contours or "form-lines", drawn as dashed lines, are some-times mapped at 7.5 metres to show additional information.

ADVANTAGES:
- Especially made for leisure use and show all the features of use to a runner or walker, whereas OS maps serve many other purposes, and show a lot of political, historical and geographical information which is of little use to the runner.
- Drawn using line thicknesses and colours which are easy to read during a competition.
- Generally up to date and consistent.
- Printed on Duxbak paper which is semiwaterproof and can be read on the fold lines.

DISADVANTAGES:
- It may take a while to get used to Harvey maps, especially for long-time users of OS maps.

MAP HINTS:
- Fences and walls are only shown on the open fell, not within farmland.
- Fields are shown as yellow, rough pasture as pale yellow.
- Paths, streams, ponds, marshes and peat hags are well shown.
- Individual boulders and sheepfolds are usually shown.
- Areas of complex detail are well shown by the accurate contours.
- Forest is shown as light green, dense forest as dark green. Firebreaks are well mapped.
- The duxbak paper is not totally indestructable and is easily stained, so the map should be laminated or put in a map case.
- Contour lines are drawn in grey where they cross rocky ground.

2 USING A MAP – THE BASICS

SETTING THE MAP WITH THE GROUND

The first principle of map reading! When looking at a map always make sure that it is lined up, or orientated, with the features on the ground. To do this, turn the map so that a feature on the map is aligned in the same direction as the same feature on the ground. This means that if you are running east, say, then the eastern side of the map will be furthest away from you. Setting the map automatically gets things "round the right way", and makes it easier to understand the map information. (The map can also be set with the compass. This is explained later).

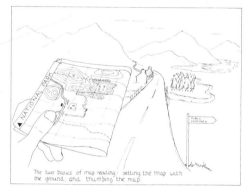

The two basics of map reading: setting the map with the ground, and thumbing the map.

THUMBING THE MAP

The second principle of map reading! Keep your thumb right next to where you are on the map. You will have to fold the map to a fairly small size in order to do this. In this way you will be able to focus on the right part of the map at a glance.

CARRYING THE MAP

During mountain marathons or navigation fell races, a good map reader will hold the map in their hand for virtually the whole of a race, in order to constantly refer to it. The only time the map should be shoved into a pocket is when you need to use both hands, for example when scrambling over rocky ground or when unwrapping a Mars bar!

3 COPYING DOWN A COURSE

USING MASTER MAPS

Before a competition you may have to copy down the course from a master map. The best way of marking the site of a checkpoint (or control, as they are sometimes called) onto a map is with a circle of about 6 to 10mm in diameter. The checkpoint feature should be at the centre of the circle. Care should be taken to avoid obscuring any map detail. If you have to visit the checkpoints in a certain order it is best to number them on the map in that order. Joining the circles with straight lines also helps you to remember which order to visit them in, and sometimes makes it easier when choosing between possible routes. A triangle is usually used to mark the start, and a double circle to mark the finish. Everyone, at some time or other, has made the disastrous mistake of copying a checkpoint in the wrong place, so it is always worth double checking at the master maps.

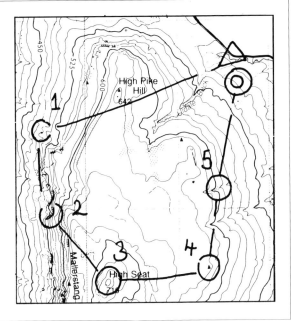

A course copied from a master map. The lines have been broken in places to avoid obscuring map detail. A triangle has been used to show the start and a double circle to show the finish
© Harveys

12

PLOTTING GRID REFERENCES

It is more usual to receive your course in the form of grid references. These are almost always given as six figures, written, for example, as 668218 or 668/218. The first three figures locate the position of the checkpoint along an east-west axis, the second three figures along a north-south axis. The illustration shows you how to plot a grid reference.

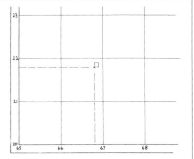

plotting a point from the grid reference 668218. 668 refers to its position on the E/W axis, and 218 to the N/S axis. The point lies within a 100m square to the NE of the intersection of 668 and 218.

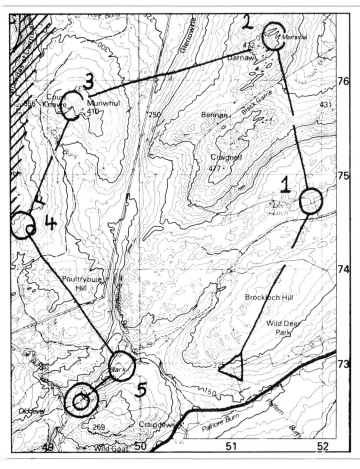

A course plotted from grid references. Can you spot the two mistakes that have been made?
© Harveys

10km, 230m climb

S	FENCE CORNER	510729
1	LOCH E.END	518747
2	MEMORIAL	514764
3	SADDLE	495755
4	FENCE BEND	487744
5	LOCH NE END	498729
F	ON THE TRACK	504726

13

The point that you plot marks the south-western corner of a 100 metre square; the checkpoint will lie within this square. A properly planned course will have checkpoints sited on features which are shown on the map, accompanied by a written description of each site. So there should be a feature at the grid reference which matches the written description. Again, mark the checkpoints with circles, number them in order and link them with straight lines. Double check everything and, if you are running as a pair, get your partner to check as well.

CHECKPOINT MARKERS

Checkpoints in fell races are almost always manned. Competitors log through each checkpoint either by having their race number taken or by handing in a numbered token. Keep your eyes open for a person or a group of people, often shouting encouragement or mild abuse! Checkpoints in mountain marathons are usually marked with standard orienteering-type markers. These are 3-sided 'kites' of orange and white nylon, about 30cm square. Competitors log through by marking a control card (that they carry round the course) with a needle punch. Checkpoints are often manned and the marshals' tent is usually a lot more obvious than the marker! Despite this it is always safer to assume that the checkpoint you are looking for will not be manned.

At the checkpoint

4 THE COMPASS

Navigation is essentially a combination of map and compass. On featureless moorland or in the mist the compass assumes a vital role and the map may be of only limited use. In clear weather, in well-defined terrain, it may be possible to navigate by map reading alone, however the compass should still be used as a back up.

It is easy to learn the simple procedures involved in using a compass - much easier than it is to learn to read a map. Yet the majority of mistakes that people make are caused by ignoring the compass. The compass is always right, except in the most exceptional circumstances, whereas a lot can, and does, go wrong with map reading.

Three methods of using the compass are described here.

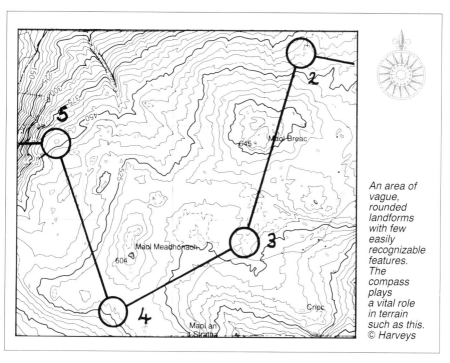

An area of vague, rounded landforms with few easily recognizable features. The compass plays a vital role in terrain such as this. © Harveys

15

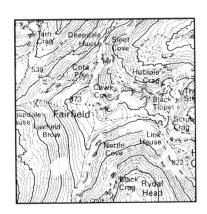

The summit of Fairfield in the Lake District. In the mist the compass may be the only way of finding the right descent route.
© Harveys

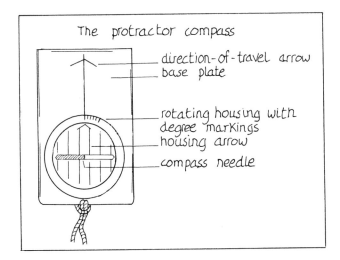

SETTING THE MAP WITH THE COMPASS

This simple technique helps with map reading and at the same time tells you which direction to run in.

Earlier on it was explained how to set the map with the ground (the first principle of map reading) by lining up the map with visible features on the ground. The map can also be set with the compass, by turning the map until the north lines (meridians) are aligned with the needle of the compass. An imaginary line on the map, drawn between you and your destination, will be pointing in the direction you need to follow.

Although this is a simple technique it can be used in almost every situation, and some competitors rarely bother with the more complicated methods of using a compass, such as taking a bearing.

16

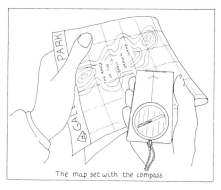

The map set with the compass

TAKING A BEARING

At first, taking a bearing may seem a complex process, and it is best practiced before trying it out in a competition! It is most useful when a high level of accuracy is needed, for example in thick mist or when trying to locate a small feature, especially when the map is of little help.

The four-stage method of taking a bearing using a modern protractor-type compass is shown in the diagram.

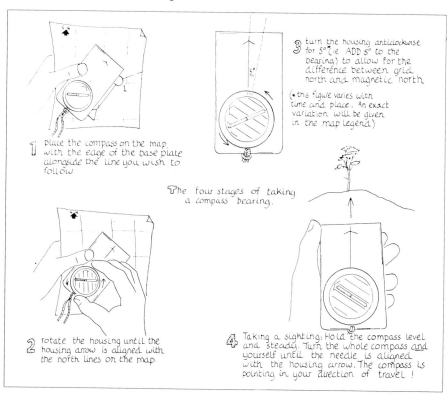

③ turn the housing anticlockwise for 5° (ie ADD 5° to the bearing) to allow for the difference between grid north and magnetic north

(*this figure varies with time and place. An exact variation will be given in the map legend)

① place the compass on the map, with the edge of the base plate alongside the line you wish to follow

The four stages of taking a compass bearing.

② rotate the housing until the housing arrow is aligned with the north lines on the map.

④ Taking a sighting: Hold the compass level and steady. Turn the whole compass and yourself until the needle is aligned with the housing arrow. The compass is pointing in your direction of travel!

17

The accuracy of your bearing depends on the care you take in making sightings from the compass, once the compass has been set. Hold the compass as level and as steady as possible. Sight along the direction arrow of the compass and choose an object such as a tree or a rock to serve as a marker that you can run towards. This object should be as far away as possible, it may even be, say, a summit on the horizon, well beyond your destination. In thick mist, in forest terrain, or at night it may be hard to see very far ahead, and there may be no alternative but to take frequent, careful sightings. In extremely low visibility you may have to keep sending your partner ahead to act as a marker (if you are on your own then you are in trouble!) It is possible, with some practice, to both set the compass and take sightings without stopping running, although this is only to be recommended when it is absolutely vital to save seconds, for example in a short, fast race. Ensure that the compass is held level and steady when taking a sighting on the move. Hold the compass in a level position for a few seconds before looking at it, to give the needle time to settle.

To save making a 5 degree allowance for magnetic variation each time the compass is set, many competitors draw North Lines on the map before they start, pointing 5 degrees left of grid north (ie to "magnetic north"). The compass is then set using these lines.

RUNNING ON "THE NEEDLE"

This is less painful than it sounds! In fact it is a way of saving time when using the compass. If you wish to run due north or due south then there is no need to set the compass as all you need to do is follow the compass needle, (remembering that the red end points north and the white end points south!). You can use the same principle to run due east or west (see diagram).

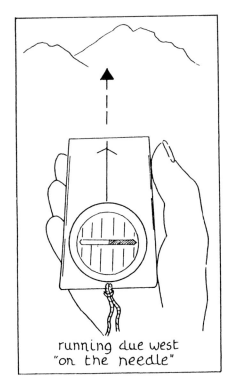

running due west
"on the needle"

TYPES OF COMPASS

The modern protractor-type compass (as illustrated in the earlier diagram) is ideal for all types of navigation. For fell racing, when the compass is only used occasionally and is usually carried in a pocket or a bumbag, a compact model is most suitable. For mountain marathons it may be worth investing in a larger model. At present the Silva type 5R is the most sophisticated (and expensive!) compass available. The 5R uses a system of mini-magnets, developed in Russia, enabling the main needle to settle almost instantly.

The "thumb-compass" is an alternative to the protractor-type compass, and, you've guessed it, it is worn on the thumb! It is held on the map at all times, keeping the map permanently set whilst showing the direction of travel, in exactly the same way that is described in the previous section on setting the map with the compass. Some models feature a rotating housing which enables you to take bearings in the same way that you would with a protractor compass. Thumb compasses require the map to be folded to a small size, which is awkward in many mountain marathons when the map is in the form of a large, laminated sheet.

When choosing a compass, bear in mind the words of an old orienteering coach; "it doesn't matter what kind you have, as long as you know how to use it".

TRUST THE COMPASS

The only time that the compass fails to do its job of pointing to the north is when you are crossing magnetic rocks, as occur in the Cuillins of Skye, or when you are standing very close to a metal object such as a steel gate or a mountain bike. These situations are very rare, and it is a safe assumption that "the compass is always right." If you are following a bearing then stick to it, even if the map seems to suggest otherwise. It rarely pays off to ignore the compass and follow a hunch; there is little evidence that human beings possess an inbuilt sense of direction! *Making steady progress*

5 DISTANCE ESTIMATION

This section deals with methods of estimating how far you have run. It has already been explained how the compass gives an accurate and reliable measure of direction. Unfortunately there is no handy instrument that gives a similar measure of distance. Knowing how far you have run is more a matter of estimation than of accurate measurement.

PACE COUNTING

Pace counting is a method of estimating the distance you have covered by keeping a mental count of the number of paces you have used. It is perhaps best to mention straight away that pace counting isn't everyones' cup of tea. Many successful competitors never use pace counting because they find that counting in their head takes away the feeling of fun and freedom that they get when running in the hills. If you feel the same then skip the rest of this section! Pace counting is not a vital part of mountain navigation in the same way that the compass is, and you can take it or leave it.

Pace counting is most useful when it is not possible to tell how far you have run by reading the features on the map. This may be because the terrain is especially featureless; for example vague, rounded moorland, or because visibility is drastically reduced by thick mist. It is also useful if you are heading for a feature, say a stream, and you suspect that there may be other unmapped streams before you get there. Pace counting is often used together with an accurate compass bearing.

Pace counting is a simple technique to learn; all you need to know is how many paces you use to cover 100 metres. You can work this out by running over a measured distance of fell-terrain at your normal race pace. Most people count double-paces, ie they only count the number of times that one of their feet touches the ground, usually the right foot. When you decide to use pace counting during a competition, you first of all need to measure the distance that you intend to cover on the map, and then work out how many paces you will use to run that distance. For example if you use 40 double-paces to cover 100m and you wish to run for 300m, then you will need to count 120 double-paces.

Some runners stick a home-made pacing scale to the base plate of their compass. This is placed on the map alongside the distance that is to be run. Gradations on the pacing scale give a measure of that distance in terms of the number of paces that the runner will use, thereby saving on mental arithmetic. A different pacing scale is needed for each different map scale. For someone who uses 40 paces per 100m, running on a map scale of 1:25000, each 10 paces will cover 25m, or 1mm on the pacing scale.

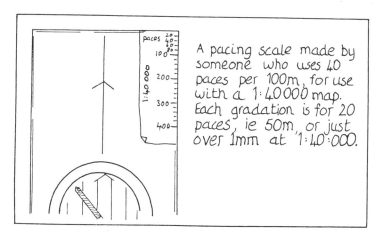

A pacing scale made by someone who uses 40 paces per 100m, for use with a 1:40000 map. Each gradation is for 20 paces, ie 50m, or just over 1mm at 1:40:000.

Perhaps the main plus-point in favour of pace counting is its potential role in mountain safety. It could provide the key to finding the safe way off a difficult mountain by, for example, helping to locate a route between crags, an abseil stake or a descent gully. It can also help the competitive runner to locate a difficult checkpoint, or to recognise a vital feature such as a path en-route to a checkpoint. On the minus-side, however, it should be remembered that pace counting is unreliable or impossible on rough or steep ground. Pace counting is perhaps best used as a last resort measure; a technique that you know how to use yet you only put into practice on those few occasions when compass and map reading do not suffice.

DISTANCE ESTIMATION BY JUDGEMENT

With practice it is possible to become skilled at recognising distances on the ground. Some people are able to look at the ground ahead and identify a feature that they judge to be, say, 100 metres away. It helps if you are, for example, a footballer who can relate 100m to the length of a football pitch, or a track athlete who knows that 100m is about the length of the finish straight. If you wished to cover 400m on the ground then you would have to divide this into four estimated lengths of 100m. This technique is of little use in thick mist when visibility can be as low as 10m!
Some people take this method a step further and estimate distance purely by feeling. They look at a distance on the map and set off running until they feel that they have gone far enough. To do this well obviously requires a great deal of practice. It is essential to develop a "feel" for the particular map scale that you are using, and this is only achieved with plenty of experience.

6 ROUTE CHOICE

Choosing a good route is one way in which the crafty tortoise can put one over on the speedy hare! Whether you see it as a fascinating challenge or a necessary evil, route choice is a vital part of mountain navigation. A good course setter will try to keep the runners on their toes by ensuring that there is route choice in almost every leg of the course.

FACTORS IN ROUTE CHOICE

When choosing a route, first of all have a good look at the map to pick out every possible option. It is worth considering even those routes that make a huge detour from the straight line. The best route may even involve setting off in a direction directly away from the checkpoint that you are trying to reach!

For each option you will have to consider the distance you will run and weigh it up against any factors that may effect your running speed. These factors may include;

- the height climbed on the route
- how much of the route is on paths or roads
- whether you will have to make any very steep climbs
- the roughness of the terrain underfoot; for example you may expect to be slowed by tussocks and marshes in a valley floor, by bracken and rocks on valley sides, or you may be able to predict fast running on the ridge tops.
- the weather, especially the wind direction
- obstacles such as crags, forest, lakes or out-of-bounds areas.
- how tired you are feeling
- how easy it is to navigate along each route
- whether you will pass a pub on the way!

To complicate things further, the fastest route may not always be the best. A long, level route along paths may be, say, 10 minutes slower, but runners taking that route will arrive at the checkpoint relatively fresh and warm and will have had a chance to plan ahead and eat some food. Runners who followed a quicker route over rugged mountain terrain may reach the checkpoint cold, disorganised and in a state of exhaustion!

agree on each route choice with your partner

22

SOME RULES OF THUMB - BOB'S LAW

Bob's Law compares the distance of a particular route with the distance of the straight line route. It is not especially exact, and mathematically-minded readers may wish to make their own refinements.

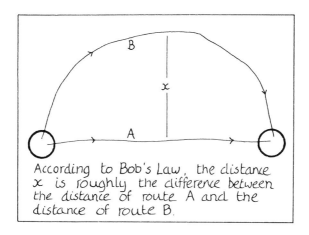

According to Bob's Law, the distance x is roughly the difference between the distance of route A and the distance of route B.

The furthest distance between the lines followed by A and B is 1.5 kilometres. By a convenient rule of geometry this happens to be roughly the amount that B is longer than A, assuming that A follows a fairly smooth curve. (When making an estimate of distance it helps to remember that grid lines are always 1 kilometre apart).

ESTIMATING HEIGHT GAIN

A popular way of doing this is to count the number of Index Contours (the thicker brown lines) crossed whilst climbing. The number of Index Contours crossed can be compared for each alternative route. Each Index Contour represents a climb of 50 metres, or 160 feet, on OS maps, and 75 metres, or 240 feet, on Harvey maps.

COMPARING DISTANCE TO HEIGHT GAIN

A rough rule is that 100 metres of ascent is equivalent to 1 kilometre of extra running. (Though this figure is open to debate!)
So a climb of one Index Contour, or 50 metres on an OS map, is equivalent to 500m extra running. This rough formula is used in the map example overleaf.

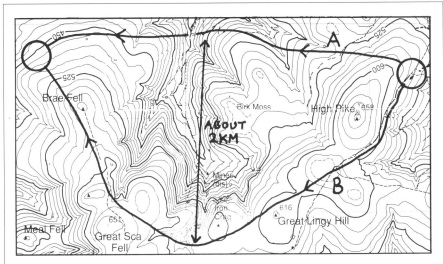

The distance between the lines of route A and route B is about 2km (or 2 grid lines). So, according to Bob's Law, B is about 2km longer than A. However A climbs an extra 10 contours (2 index contours) or 150m. 150m climb is roughly equivalent to 1.5km running on the flat, so A looks the better route.
© Harveys

JUDGEMENT BASED ON EXPERIENCE

It has to be said that the above rules of thumb only provide a rough estimate, and do not take into account many factors, not least of which is the time taken to do the sums! If, like the author, you find that performing feats of mental arithmetic takes some of the pleasure out of running, then you will be pleased to learn that judgement and experience are often the best ways of choosing the quickest route! With experience you may be able to tell from a glance at the map which is the best route. By taking an overview of the whole leg it is sometimes possible to pick out a good natural line, linking sections of fast running and avoiding major climbs. With a knowledge of the mountains, especially of the area you are running in, you may be able to predict, say, that there will be deep tussocks on lower ground or heather on the ridges.

tussocks in the glens......scree on the slopes...... heather on the ridges... ...I'll be choosing a route to the nearest bar!!

A leg from the B course of the Karrimor in 1989. At a glance, route A is the more obvious and appears to involve less climb as it follows a series of ridges. Route B makes a large descent and ascent and looks the hillier. Counting the index contours reveals that in fact both routes climb about 4.5 index contours. As both routes are about the same distance there is probably little between them, although B follows a less exposed line and may be a better bet in wild, windy weather.
© Harveys

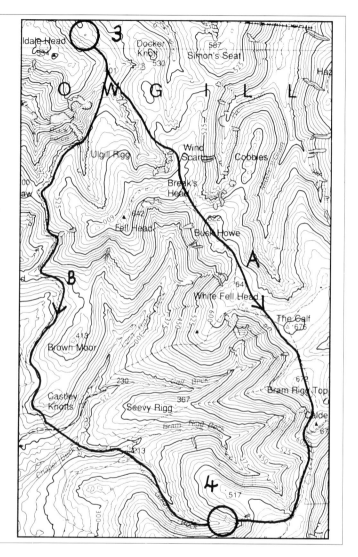

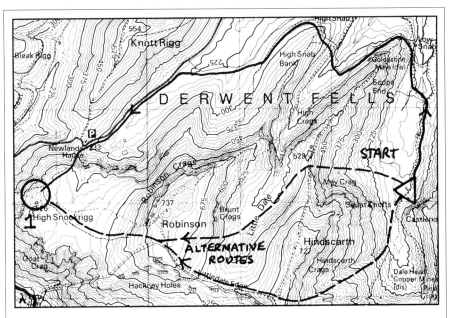

Leg 1 from day 2 of the Karrimor C course, Threlkeld 1992.
James Brown describes the route that won him the race: "We were off a few seconds
behind the leaders in the chasing start. We never saw where they went as it was still
dark and a blizzard was blowing. No. 1 looked a hard leg so we huddled behind a
boulder to think about it. We saw a good route back past the campsite. It looked about
2km longer than the alternatives but it had about 200m less climb. It looked to be fast
running on paths and roads, had an easy approach to the checkpoint and would give
us a chance to get sorted out and plan routes for the rest of the course. Most
importantly it was sheltered, and my partner refused to go "up those bloody mountains
at this time of day!" Ours were the first footprints on the route. When we got to No. 1 we
had a 12 minute lead and we had avoided dying of hypothermia!"
© Harveys

26

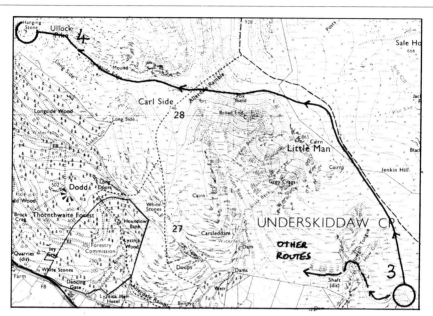

Mark Seddon, elite winner, describes his route: "1991 Capricorn day 1 - an excellent course planned by Mike Walford. Everyone was taking an easy contouring path out of No. 3, but this forced a low route crossing very steep slopes and gullies. I decided that an up-and-over route would in fact have less climb and, just as important, be faster running. I took 38 minutes - the other route took about 10 minutes longer". Mark was not tempted by the contouring path leaving No 3 as he had looked at the WHOLE leg when planning his route and realised that, painful as it was, it was better to make the steep climb out of the checkpoint. He also observed: "It is easy to get carried away with 'saving some height' by taking a contouring route. Very often the so-called contouring route has more climb than any other route, although this may be hidden in a series of short ascents".

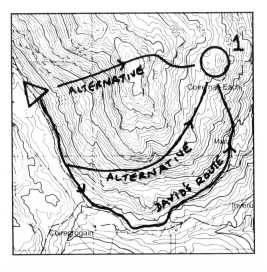

The first leg of the elite course on day 2 of the 1991 Karrimor at Arrochar. David Rosen, a runner who rarely misses a mountain marathon, and usually finishes amongst the leading teams, describes the route he took with Andy Lewsley: "The 2km leg was a classic over-or-round problem. For Andy and myself the choice was clear. Even though the track route was more than twice as far as the straight line, it saved about 1000 feet of climbing and would be easy going until the radio mast. In addition, attacking the checkpoint from the top of the mist covered mountain would be no easy matter." David in fact caught the leaders on this leg.
© Harveys

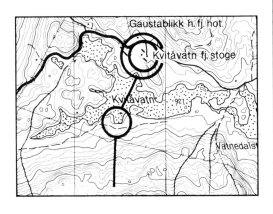

The last leg of a Norwegian mountain marathon. The British team of Carol McNeill and Ros Coates swam the lake and gained some places!

EYEBALLS, MAN!!

An orienteering instructor and major in the Marines often startled his young charges by bellowing out; "Eyeballs, Man, Use Your Bloody Eyeballs!!". He would go on to explain that its all very well to be skilled with a map and compass, but do not forget to look at the ground immediately in front of you in order to choose a good line through the terrain. It may be possible to avoid marshes, rocks and heather, or to pick up areas of level ground or sheep tracks. This all sounds fairly obvious, but the art of "reading the terrain" is a part of route choice that can only be improved with practice.

7 ROUTE CHOICE FOR SCORE CLASSES

Several events in the mountain marathon calender include score classes in which competitors are given the locations of a large number of checkpoints and must visit as many as possible within a set time limit. Checkpoints may be visited in any order, and each checkpoint has a points value. There are usually heavy points penalties for exceeding the time limit. The Karrimor International Mountain Marathon offers two score classes: the Long Score with a time limit of 7 hours on the first day and 6 on the second day, and the Short Score with slightly shorter time limits. Score classes have become increasingly popular with competitors who enjoy the additional challenge of deciding in which order to visit the checkpoints. Other competitors prefer score classes because they know how long they are likely to spend out each day. Perhaps the main advantage of score classes is that they offer a wide variety of different routes, and as a result there are few of the "crocodiles" of runners on the same route that are too often a feature of mountain marathons.

The Klets Classic Course at the Saunders Lakeland Mountain Marathon works in a similar way, however although the checkpoints may be visited in any order, they must all be visited in the shortest time.

PREPARATION BEFORE THE EVENT

Before you start, it helps to know how far you are able to run in the allocated time limit. You may be able to work out an approximate figure from the times you have taken in previous events. For example, if you have recently run a 24km course in 8 hours, then in a 6 hour score class you should cover about 18km or, to be on the safe side, say 16km. You should also make allowances for the expected roughness and hilliness of the terrain. It is useful to bear in mind that very few people travel faster than 5km per hour in mountain marathons, and most travel at about 3.5km per hour.

When you are planning a route on the start line you should roughly measure its distance, perhaps by using the end of your compass which may be, say, 2.5km at map scale. So 6 compass widths equals 15km. This need only take a few seconds. It may help to remember that grid lines are 1km apart, and that every tenth grid line is drawn with a thicker line. Some competitors carry a piece of string which, when placed on the map, corresponds to the distance they expect to cover.

Setting off!

CHOOSING A ROUTE

You should not set off from the start before you have planned out, at least in rough, which checkpoints you will visit and in what order. It is worth taking an overview of the whole map, as quite often a good route, following natural lines in the terrain, quickly springs to mind. As with any route choice decision, it is important to consider factors such as height climb and ease of running when choosing the order - the shortest route between the checkpoints may not be the quickest. In addition you have to bear in mind the points value carried by each checkpoint; is it worth the gamble of going for a high value, but remote, checkpoint? Perhaps the best preparation for a score event is to have your brain replaced with a computer!

THE "OPTIONS" STRATEGY

The key to success in score classes is to reach the finish at just the right time. If you finish late you will incur heavy penalties, whereas if you finish early you may have missed out on potential points. A popular and effective strategy is to divide your route into two parts before you set off from the start. The first part, about 50% to 75% of the route, involves sticking closely to a pre-chosen plan. During this stage you can forget about the order of visiting the checkpoints, as this has already been decided, and fully concentrate on the navigation required to find each checkpoint. The second part is chosen to include a number of options, which can be taken depending on how much time is left. It is convenient if there is a cluster of low-value checkpoints near the finish which can be left until last. You can then visit a few, all, or none of them depending on how much time is left.

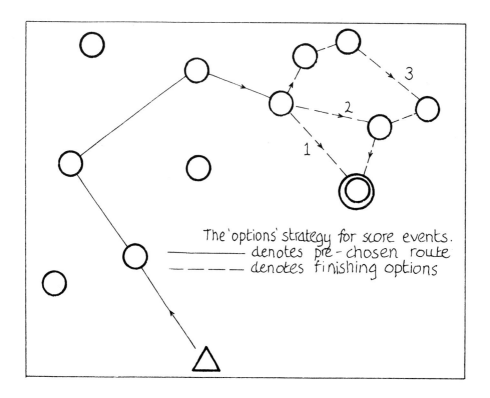

The 'options' strategy for score events.
———— denotes pre-chosen route
— — — — denotes finishing options

8 ROUGH NAVIGATION

Rough navigation is a term describing those techniques that are used when your aim is to cover a lot of ground as quickly as possible, for example on a long leg when you want to get somewhere close to the next checkpoint without making any unnecessary hesitations on the way there. Nearer the checkpoint it is usually wise to slow down and take more care. The techniques used when near the checkpoint are termed "fine navigation" and are dealt with in the next section.

ROUGH MAP READING

The art of rough navigation lies in simplifying things; in other words just using the largest, most easily recognised features. It is easy to waste time by trying to read too much of the information on the map.

At the start of a leg, look at the map and decide which are the major features that you are likely to follow or cross. They may be streams, walls, ridges, valleys etc. Tick these off as you pass them on the ground. If you happen to run past any small features that tell you exactly where you are then this is a bonus, but it is important not to waste any time by setting out to look for such features.

rough navigation

With practice it is possible to master the skill of reading the map without stopping running - but watch out for large cliffs!

ROUGH COMPASS

The use of the compass in rough navigation is to keep you heading in the right direction whilst you map read by the larger features. The compass is vital as without it you would have to read more from the map in order to navigate and this would slow you down. The compass may be used in any of the ways described earlier in this booklet, for example to take a bearing or for running on the needle.

With practice it is possible to take sightings from the compass whilst on the run. This is a useful skill in the hectic atmosphere of a fell race, but is less applicable to Mountain Marathons, where things move at a more genteel pace!

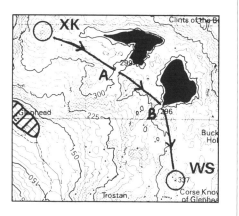

A leg from the C course of the Rock+Run in Galloway in 1989. Rough navigation can be used to reach B; ie following rough compass, using just the general shape of the ground, noting the stream at A and trying not to waste time by reading the smaller features. Point B, at the stream leaving the loch, is a good, obvious attack point from which to start fine navigation, (described in the next section).
© Harveys

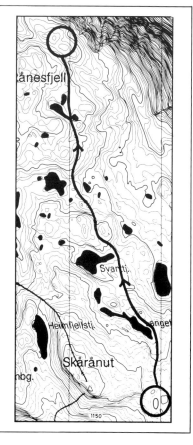

Rough navigation in Norwegian terrain. This route follows a good natural line, with the many tarns and larger summits providing points of reference.

33

9 FINE NAVIGATION

The term "fine navigation" describes a combination of techniques which may be used at one of the key parts of a course when it is necessary to navigate with extreme care. Course setters often try to make things difficult by siting a checkpoint in an area of broken, complex terrain, for example amongst the tarns and hummocks of Haystacks in the Lake District, or in the glaciated granite knolls of the Dungeon Hills of Galloway.

Assuming that the ground is well represented on the map, this presents a fair challenge, and a canny competitor will always be able to locate the checkpoint without losing time.

Other situations which require a careful approach occur, for example, when a checkpoint is sited on a small feature in an otherwise featureless area, when a checkpoint is sited in a forest, or when a checkpoint is approached across a steep slope.

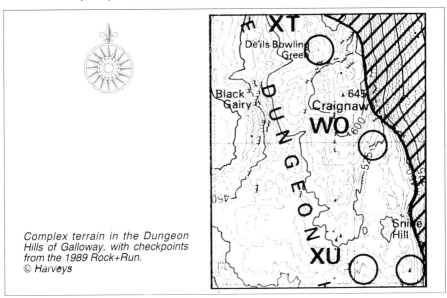

Complex terrain in the Dungeon Hills of Galloway, with checkpoints from the 1989 Rock+Run.
© Harveys

IDENTIFYING A DIFFICULT CHECKPOINT

The first stage of fine navigation is to spot potentially difficult parts of the course before you get there. Experience helps in this, however as a general rule anything sited well away from a large feature may be hard to find, especially if the checkpoint feature is itself small, and is located on a steep slope, or in the middle of nowhere, or amidst a mass of other small, similar features.

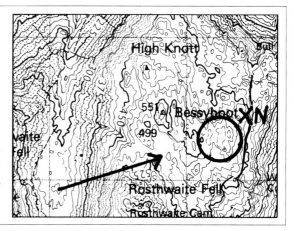

A checkpoint sited in particularly complex terrain from the Rock+Run elite course in 1988. The wall 200m beyond the checkpoint provides a useful 'collecting feature' in the event of over-shooting.
©Harveys

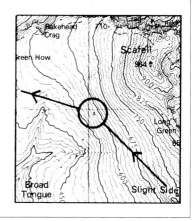

A checkpoint made doubly difficult by its situation on a small feature (a sheepfold) in an otherwise featureless area, and by the approach which follows a diagonally downhill line.
© Harveys

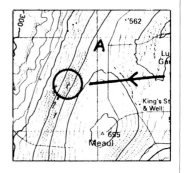

This checkpoint on the crag foot could well prove tricky, as crags are hard to spot from above. In addition, missing a checkpoint on a steep slope often results in the loss of much time and energy. It may be worth using the fence junction at A as a definite "attack point" from which to approach the checkpoint.
© Harveys

CHANGING FROM ROUGH TO FINE NAVIGATION

When approaching a difficult checkpoint there will come a time when you feel it is necessary to make the transition from full-steam-ahead rough navigation to careful fine navigation. You may choose a large, obvious feature, or ATTACK POINT, from which to begin fine navigating. This should be as near to the checkpoint as possible, and, as it has to be located using rough navigation techniques, it must be something that you can rely on finding, such as a tarn or trig point. In practice, however, the transition from rough to fine navigation may be gradual, with no definite attack point.

FINE NAVIGATION TECHNIQUES

Having decided that a checkpoint is difficult, you should use every technique available, in combination, in order to find it. Speed is relatively unimportant, so it does not matter if you have to slow down in order to concentrate on the navigation.

SLOWING DOWN

Forcing yourself to slow down in order to find a tricky checkpoint can be the hardest part of fine navigation, especially in the heat of the moment with other runners around you. It takes some discipline to say to yourself "right, this looks hard, now I'm going to slow down and concentrate", but remember that the other runners probably have little idea what they are looking for and could well end up rushing around in the hope of getting lucky! In a mountain marathon they may even be on a different course to you.

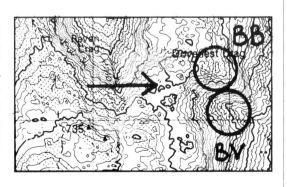

Checkpoint BB was visited by Kirkfell class runners at the 1992 Saunders, whereas BV was visited by the Carrock Fell class.
Unfortunately a number of teams were disqualified for visiting the wrong checkpoint. They were perhaps pressured by other teams into not slowing down enough, ignoring the map and using following tactics!
© Harveys

FINE COMPASS

The most accurate way to use a compass is to take a bearing (see the previous section on the compass) but make sure that you stand still and take care when taking each sighting. The compass should be used in every fine navigation situation.

If the terrain is complex and well-mapped then the compass will serve as an important back-up to map reading. When heading for a small feature in vague terrain the compass is vital.

FINE MAP READING

The idea behind fine map reading is to maintain "continuous contact" with the map by reading every feature that you pass. This is difficult and takes some practice, as you have to have a good feel for the scale of the map and you have to know how features are likely to be represented on the map. Above all, you should have a good look at the contours on the map and use them to form a mental picture of the shape of the ground. Other features such as crags, streams and marshes are often less reliably mapped but provide useful extra information. The next chapter explains the use of contours in more detail. Having a good mental picture of the ground is especially important when approaching the checkpoint itself. You should know what feature the checkpoint is on, and have an idea of what the ground will look like before, on either side, and beyond the checkpoint.

Keep checking the compass when fine map reading. You may lose contact with the map for a while, but by staying on a bearing you will know that you are still on line, and hopefully you will be able to locate your position later on.

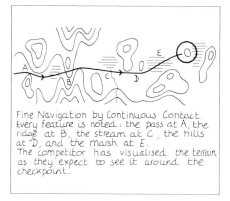

Fine Navigation by Continuous Contact. Every feature is noted: the pass at A, the ridge at B, the stream at C, the hills at D, and the marsh at E. The competitor has visualised the terrain as they expect to see it around the checkpoint.

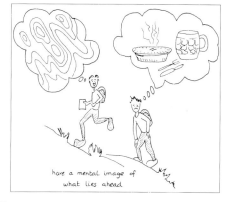

have a mental image of what lies ahead

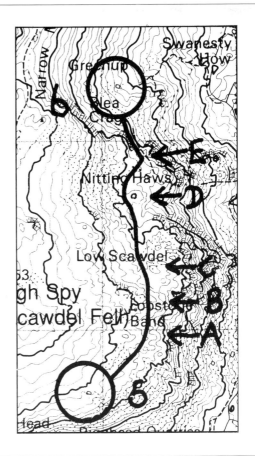

Continuous Contact Map Reading

Leg 5 to 6 from day 1 of the C course at the 1992 Karrimor. James Brown describes his route: "We wanted to find the path at E which led through the crags almost to the checkpoint. We had to read the map all the way to stay on line. We traversed out of No. 5, crossed the ridges at A and B then dropped to the knoll at C and followed a stream downhill. We ran behind the prominent knoll at D, then onto the ridge at E to pick up the path".
© Harveys

A checkpoint from the B course of the Karrimor at Arrochar in 1991. Claire of the 'Banditos' team describes how she found it using fine navigation techniques: We were very careful because of the thick mist and because the checkpoint looked difficult. We knew where we were at A, and from B we took a compass bearing. We deliberately aimed to the south of the crag where the contours show a steep slope. When we hit this we turned north.....and there it was! This technique is known as 'aiming-off'. Missing the crag to the north could have resulted in the loss of a lot of time.
© Harveys

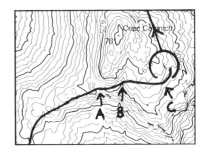

10 UNDERSTANDING CONTOURS

Understanding contours is the key to successful navigation. Contours show the ground as a complete picture; both the layout of the main hills and valleys, and the intricacies of areas of smaller features. Contours never change or become out-of-date as a map gets older, whereas footpaths alter, streams and marshes vary with the season, and forests are planted or felled. Unfortunately contours are the hardest part of the map to understand, as they require you to imagine a 3-dimensional landscape in your head, based only on the brown squiggles on a piece of paper.

WHAT ARE CONTOURS?

A contour is a line joining points of equal height. Contours show the height, steepness and shape of the ground.

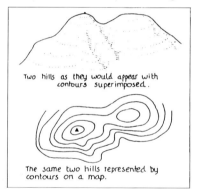

Two hills as they would appear with contours superimposed.

The same two hills represented by contours on a map.

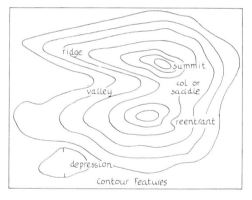

Contour Features

WHAT IS UP AND WHAT IS DOWN?

When you pick up a map of an unfamiliar area for the first time it is easy to confuse ridges with valleys and "ups" with "downs". Before you start racing it is a good idea to get a rough picture of the area in your mind. When working out the ups and downs, remember that Index Contours (the thicker lines) are numbered to show their height above sea level. In addition there are usually streams in the valley floors, tarns lie in hollows and lakes in valley floors. Closed contours encircle summits or higher ground, trig points and cairns are usually sited on summits or ridges, and, on a Harvey map, the tags on crags point downslope.

UNDERSTANDING FINE CONTOUR DETAIL

Course setters love to site checkpoints in areas of lumps, bumps, hillocks and hollows. The summit of Bessyboot in Borrowdale is one such area, as are parts of the Rhinog Mountains in Wales. Far from being a meaningless mess, however, the contours in such areas are usually well mapped. The contours on Harvey maps and modern OS maps have been plotted from air photos and show the ground extremely well. The smallest squiggle in a line will show the position of a tiny hollow or bump on a hillside, and it is quite possible to navigate by features such as these. Maps of such accuracy have only become available recently, and many experienced hill-users, used to old-style OS maps, may be unaware that they can pinpoint their position on the smallest features, or map read through areas of complex terrain.

IMPROVING CONTOUR READING

The only way to learn and get better at using contours is to spend a lot of time on the hills with a map. It helps to get a good "feel for the map", so that you can judge what a 10 metre or a 15 metre contour interval looks like on the ground. When practising with a map you should look at the way in which features are mapped; for example how does a one-contour hill compare in size with a two-contour hill? When is a feature too small to be shown? Some exercises for improving map reading are described later in this book.

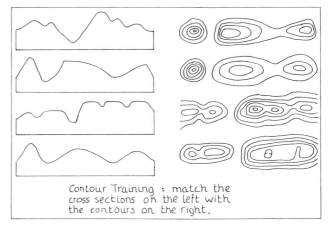

Contour Training : match the cross sections on the left with the contours on the right.

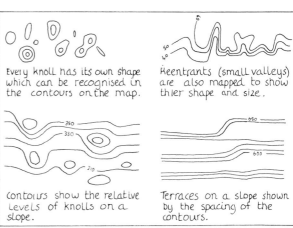

Every knoll has its own shape which can be recognised in the contours on the map.

Reentrants (small valleys) are also mapped to show thier shape and size.

Contours show the relative levels of knolls on a slope.

Terraces on a slope shown by the spacing of the contours.

11 RELOCATION –
or what to do when you get lost!

Getting lost can be an unpleasant experience.....things seem to be going well for a while until you gradually become aware that the map does not quite match the ground.....you know you are near the checkpoint but you don't know which way to turn .... All the time the clock is ticking on, and a growing feeling of frustration and panic makes it hard to keep a cool head. In this situation, which is surely familiar to everyone, it helps to have a ready made plan of action. Certainly any positive strategy is better than running around aimlessly.

Relocation is a skill in its own right. Even the best navigators get lost surprisingly often, however many have perfected the art of finding out where they are so that their mistakes cost them very little time.

This section looks at two different plans of action for relocation. These are illustrated by the two flowcharts below. The first of these is for use when you are lost in "mid-leg", in other words when you are still a long way from the next checkpoint. The second strategy is for use when you are lost somewhere close to the next checkpoint.

Don't Panic! Think clearly

Are you trying to follow a straight-line route with no major obstacles such as deep valleys or crags?

YES — Keep moving confidently on your original compass bearing until you see a feature which can be identified on the map

NO — Stop. Set the map with the compass and try to match it to the ground

STILL LOST?

try to relocate by remembering the features you saw before getting lost

STILL LOST?

Can you see any distant features on which to take a back-bearing?

STILL LOST?

Continue in roughly the direction of the checkpoint until you see a recognisable feature

RELOCATION IN MID-LEG

MID-LEG RELOCATION

A plan of action! Mid-leg relocation on Blea Rigg in the Lake District. "At point A I realised that I didn't have a clue where I was! But I was confident in my compass bearing and kept going without slowing down. When I saw the steep slope at B I knew where I was and cruised into the checkpoint!'
© Harveys

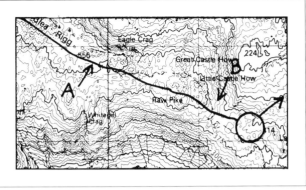

Stay cool !

Set the map with the compass. Will it now fit the ground ?

STILL LOST ?

Try to recall the features you saw before getting lost

STILL LOST ?

Is there a large feature nearby such as a path, fence or river?

YES   NO

Head straight to that feature to relocate, then re-plan a route to the checkpoint

Oh Dear !

Decide where the checkpoint is most likely to be. Head in that direction, keeping the map set with the compass, until you see an identifiable feature

RELOCATION NEAR THE CHECKPOINT

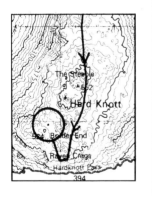

RELOCATION NEAR THE CHECKPOINT

Relocation near the checkpoint on Hard Knott Fell in the Lake District. "After The Steeple the map just didn't make any sense even though I knew the checkpoint was somewhere nearby. Rather than run around aimlessly, I headed south until I could see the road at the top of the pass, then went back carefully. I could have gone back to The Steeple to relocate, but I guessed this might involve more running."
© Harveys

42

This map section shows the route taken by David Rosen and Jon Broxap at the first checkpoint on the elite course on day 2 of the 1992 Karrimor at Threlkeld. They were unlucky to cross the stream at No. 1 at a point where it was obscured by deep snow. David describes the process of relocation: "Jon had a look at the map and agreed we must have overshot. We headed down and back - we had to relocate on the main stream somehow. The best bet seemed to be to find the sheepfold. This was no easy matter in the deep snow. We then pace counted up the main stream until we found the very faint line of the stream we were looking for."
© Harveys

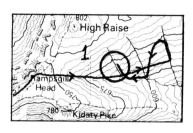

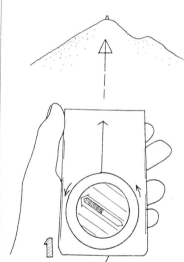

Take a sighting on a distant feature that you have identified on the map. Turn the housing until the housing arrow is aligned with the north needle.
Then subtract about 5° from the bearing for magnetic variation. (Do not confuse this with taking a bearing from the map, when the 5° is added).

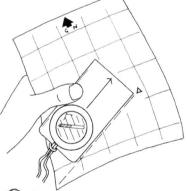

2 Place the compass on the map so that the feature you sighted on is on the edge of the base plate. Turn the compass so the the housing arrow is aligned with the north lines on the map. Your position will be somewhere on a line along the side of the base plate, passing through the feature that you sighted on

TAKING A BACK-BEARING: a useful technique if you are lost but you can recognise a distant feature.

12 TRAINING FOR IMPROVEMENT

Like any practical skill, navigation is best learned through experience. To become "fluent" with a map is similar to becoming fluent at a language. With a lot of practice you will be able to look at the map and form an instant mental picture of the ground, but before you reach this stage you will have to go through a process of "translation" in your mind.

Unfortunately, for many runners there is little opportunity to get out and practice navigation. In the mountain marathon calender there are only three or four events each year, and for many it is a long drive to the hills to find suitable terrain. For those with the chance, however, it is well worth making the effort to do some technique training, either alone or with some friends.

It is hard to improve simply by running in competitions; under the pressure of a race and in the heat of the moment it is all too easy to revert to old bad habits. It is better to learn things in the less stressful atmosphere of an informal training session - at the very least its a good excuse to get out on the hills!

SOME TRAINING EXERCISES

The following map sections are intended to give some ideas for training exercises. Please do not run the actual courses shown here as they are all on private land.

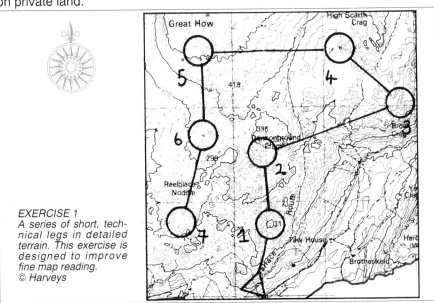

EXERCISE 1
A series of short, technical legs in detailed terrain. This exercise is designed to improve fine map reading.
© Harveys

44

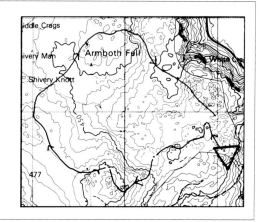

EXERCISE 2
A line exercise. Following the line as closely as possible is excellent training for continuous contact map reading.
© *Harveys*

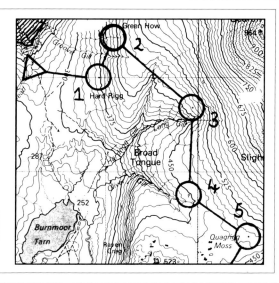

EXERCISE 3
Part of a compass training exercise. A series of short legs between small features in otherwise featureless terrain.
© *Harveys*

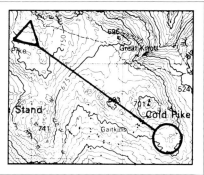

EXERCISE 4
A relocation exercise. A pair of runners use only one map. One runner navigates about halfway along the leg then hands over the map to his partner who has to complete the route.
© *Harveys*

45

EXERCISES TO DO AT HOME

Plot a course on a map - descriptions of old courses are often given in the back of results booklets, for example from the Karrimor and the OS Mountain Trial. Take the map out with you on a run and try to work out the best route choices. You can combine this with an interval session or a hill session. After each repetition give yourself, say, two minutes to work out the best route Alternatively get a friend to plan you a course whilst you plan a course for them. Then swap maps and work out the best routes. Planning a course is in itself a good form of training. With some imagination, these exercises can be varied endlessly.

TRY ORIENTEERING

The sport of orienteering, whilst being great fun in its own right, provides excellent training for mountain navigation. Orienteering events take place almost every weekend, in every part of the country, so even if you live several hours from the nearest mountains, there should be an orienteering event somewhere near you. Orienteering courses are considerably shorter than most fell races and mountain marathons, being between 2 and 15 kilometres in length and taking between 20 and 120 minutes to complete. They are held in relatively small areas of forest or moorland, always using a map showing the terrain in great detail, and with many more checkpoints or "controls" than mountain marathons or fell races - usually between 10 and 25. Accurate fine navigation is at a premium, and it is easy to see why a lot of successful mountain marathoners come from an orienteering background. At an orienteering event there are always courses available for beginners, and there are usually plenty of people around eager to give advice. To find out about events near you, you can contact your local orienteering club. Club addresses are available from the British Orienteering Federation at; Riversdale, Dale Road North, Darley Dale, MATLOCK DE4 2HX.

13 NAVIGATING IN 'TRADITIONAL' FELL RACES

Most traditional fell races are held over the same course each year, usually with several compulsory checkpoints. After the event has been going for a few years the best route is well known, although many keener runners go out for a pre-race recce in the hope of finding their own personal short-cuts! These races are not generally thought of as involving navigation, however they can become notoriously tricky in misty weather when it becomes impossible to see any other runners, let alone the way ahead. Things are even harder for the race leader out in front.

World Cup Fell Racing; England versus Italy

RACE NOTES

The difference between success and disaster may hinge on the very simple measure of carrying a small compass with you and having a few bearings written on the back of your hand. You may also want to make a few notes on the course before you start. If there isn't room on the back of your hand then write the notes on a piece of paper and pin it to a wrist band. If you feel you need even more information then take a photocopied section of a map, and write on it any key pieces of information such as bearings. This can be protected with a plastic laminate and pinned to a wrist band.

PREPARING RACE NOTES

You don't need to run around the course before the race in order to prepare race notes, you just need to look at a map and, if possible, talk to some friends who have done the race before. The key pieces of information that you will need are compass bearings. You can take these from the map before you start by following the process described in the "taking a bearing" diagram in the earlier section of this handbook dealing with the compass. The compass dial will give a reading in degrees which you can then note down, and reset on the dial during the race. Remember to add about 5 degrees to allow for magnetic variation.

DON'T GO OFF TOO FAST !!

1. PATH / STREAM above S.Tarn

2. THUNACAR KNOTT
285° to Langdale Combe (path v. faint!)
then path 275° to A.Tarn then 300°

3. ESK HAUSE SHELTER
traverse esk Pike - FIND PATH!! - 155°
(~over top if v. misty).

4. BOWFELL
110° off , 300m, then 180° to three-tarns
avoid first crinkles to R. - but go over
if misty.

5. LONG TOP
160° off to end of Crinkles then 120°
down to Red Tarn then path up 75°

6. BLISCO
85° - main path to Redacre Gill - cut
off Right. (v. faint path - CARE!)

7. CATTLE GRID

An example of personal race notes drawn up for the Langdale Horseshoe Race. A magnetic allowance of about 5° has already been made to each bearing. The comments are based on memory or on gen obtained from other runners. These notes can be pinned to a wrist band for easy reference.

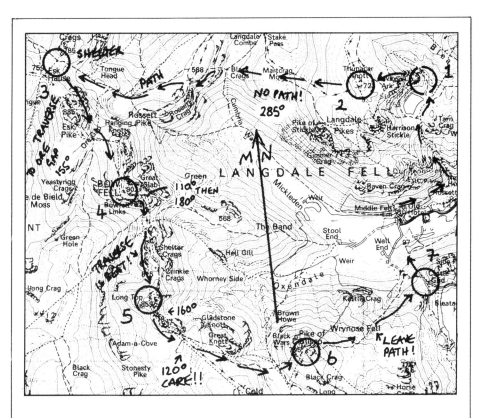

Race Notes from the Langdale Horseshoe Race drawn onto the OS 1:50000 map. A runner has prepared the map before the race in anticipation of misty conditions (a wise move, as this race is held in mid-October). Each checkpoint has been marked on the map, together with useful bearings. The runner has drawn on what they consider to be the best route, taking care to avoid obscuring any map detail. The map section can be photocopied and pinned to a wrist band or carried in a pocket together with a compass.
© Crown Copyright

PRACTICE

You need to be confident in the compass before leaving a summit and plunging down into the mist, especially if other people are going a different way. It is worth going out on a misty day and getting in some practice before using the compass in an actual race.

14 SOME COMMON MISTAKES

The map sections below illustrate a selection of commonly made mistakes. Each mistake is analysed in order to find out what went wrong. Some of the examples are made up, and others really happened to friends of the author, who were cajoled into describing their "most memorable mistake"!

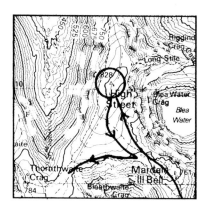

1.
The author made this mistake in the Kentmere Horseshoe Race by following a pack of runners in thick mist. The mistake was caused by not looking at map or compass (even though I had them in my pocket) and by assuming that everyone else knew where they were going. The mistake was corrected when I felt something was wrong and got out my compass.
© Harveys

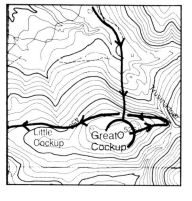

2.
The 180 degree error. A disastrous mistake, but easily made by following the compass the 'wrong way round'. Check that the compass is round the right way when you place it on the map to take a bearing. Also check that it is the north end of the needle, not the south end, that is aligned with the arrow on the compass housing when you are making a sighting.
© Harveys

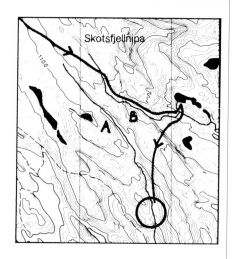

3.
A parallel error. This competitor intended to follow stream A to the checkpoint, but mistakenly followed stream B. Parallel ridges and streams are a feature of many mountain areas. Once you are on the wrong feature it is all too easy to make the map fit the ground. In this example the runner should have taken more care to pick up the right stream (after all this was the hardest section of the leg). The compass would also have shown a discrepancy in the direction of the stream.

4.
A leg from the Copeland Chase 1992. A top competitor, who should have known better, describes his mistake: "A balls-up! Firstly I chose a poor route - I didn't see the path contouring from the stream below Wandope Moss. Secondly I made a parallel error in the snow and thick mist on Grasmoor. I saw a mound and cairn and thought I was at A when infact I was at B. A path led down in what seemed to be the right direction for Lad Hows. After a couple of minutes I realised I was wrong, but I also realised I had to carry on down to make sure. I got a view of Wandope Moss and contoured (across snow-covered scree - great!) to the right ridge. Time loss 12 minutes and 5 places."
This uncharacteristic cat-alogue of errors from an experienced competitor has to be put down in part to a lapse of concentration. However more positive compass and distance estimation would have avoided the confusion between the cairns which were, after all, 500m apart.
© Crown Copyright

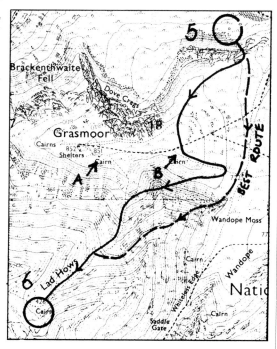

51

5 A mistake that was nipped-in-the-bud. Mark Seddon describes his route from day 2 of the 1992 Capricorn (his route is shown here on the Harvey map, although the race was in fact held on the OS 1:25000): "I was getting tired, and instead of gradually climbing over the main shoulder of Knott I crossed a lower ridge running south. A glance at the compass told me that the valley in front of me was running in the wrong direction to be Grainsgill Beck - the valley I was looking for. I was able to relocate and continue with the loss of 2 or 3 minutes. If I had descended into the wrong valley my mistake would have been much more costly."
This example shows how a good navigator can prevent an error almost before it happens. An almost subconcious part of your technique should be to keep a constant check for the possibility of something going wrong. If the map does not quite fit the ground, or the compass is pointing in slightly the wrong direction, then 'alarm bells' should start ringing. © Harveys

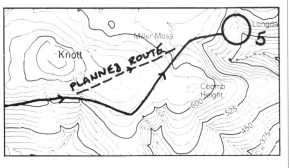

15   SAFETY

There is no single navigation technique that is vital to mountain safety, however the better you are at navigation in general, the safer you will be on the hills.

The equipment that you carry does, of course, play a key role in safety. Equipment is really beyond the scope of this handbook, however it is worth stressing the importance of keeping to the equipment rules laid down by race organisers. In addition, you should always report to the finish, whether you have completed the course or you are retiring. At every race the organisers will keep a check of who is out on the fells, and failure to report to the finish could well lead to a mountain rescue call out.

Another point worth making is that, although the organisers will do all they can to make the event as safe as possible, once you have left the start your safety is as much your own responsibility as it would be on any solo or informal trip into the hills.

16 THE GOOD RACE GUIDE

This is a list of British fell races and mountain marathons where the courses and venues are changed from year to year and where navigation skills are necessary. There are a few excellent races which are not listed here; some of these seek to keep a low profile. It is likely that there will be a number of new races starting up in the future. This is partly due to the huge demand for races of this type. It is also likely, however, that due to an increased concern for conservation there will be a larger number of smaller events in the future, rather than a few massive events as there are today.

This list does not mention the many races held abroad. The most notable of these is the Swiss Karrimor, although mountain marathons are regularly held in France, The Republic of Ireland, Scandinavia, Canada, Australia and New Zealand.

Most of the races listed here are over-subscribed and have to be entered well in advance on an entry form obtained from the organisers.

EARLY MARCH	THE NEW CHEW RACE. Chew valley. 17 miles and 3 hour score. Strictly limited entry. F. Sykes, Tame House, Delph New Road, Dobcross, Oldham OL3 5BA
MID JUNE	THE SILVA HILL RACE. In Surrey but not for softies! 5 to 15 miles on forest tracks with some big hills. Silva UK, Unit 10, Sky Business Park, Egham, Surrey TW20 8RF
JUNE LAST WEEKEND	THE CAPRICORN. Held just about anywhere! 5 classes. 25 to 50km. A 2 day event for solo runners, returning to a central campsite each day. Good courses, well organised. Capricorn, 4 Peel Place, Barrowford, Nelson, Lancs, BB9 6BE
JULY FIRST WEEKEND	THE SAUNDERS LAKELAND MM. Held in the Lake District since 1978. A good atmosphere. Beer at the mid camp and an excellent meal at the finish - the courses are OK as well! 8 courses, 30 to 60 km including the solo Klets and two for walkers. Robert Saunders Tentmakers, Five Oaks Lane, Chigwell Essex IG7 4QP

LATE JULY	THE ROHAN ROCK+RUN MM. An event which goes out of its way to find extremes of terrain and weather. Not too long, but tough and technical. Wendy Dodds, with 20 years experience of elite MMs, describes a moment from the 1988 RRMM: "We 'front pointed' up the east side of Steeple in our fell shoes!....we could see footprints in the snow and assumed others had been that way. The prints ended on a steep snow slope - we had caught up the two ice climbers who had made them! We asked them to carry on so we could use their steps...." Courses elite to short. Rohan, 30 Maryland Road, Tongwell, Milton Keynes, Bucks, MK15 8HN
MID SEPTEMBER	THE OS MOUNTAIN TRIAL. Always in the Lakes. Long courses attracting grizzled veterans of the fells. Mens 20 miles. Womens 15 miles. 838 Tring Road, Leeds LS12 5HE
MID SEPTEMBER	THE ANDERSONS MOURNE MM. Always in the Mountains of Mourne, Northern Ireland. The weekend after the OS. A, B & C classes. 40 to 65km. 18 Cranmore Gardens, Belfast BT9 6JL
OCTOBER LAST WEEKEND	THE KARRIMOR INTERNATIONAL MM. The largest and most prestigious MM. Called the "Ultimate Challenge" which perhaps refers to the awesome feat of organising 2000 competitors as much as to the courses. Now in its third decade, which is about the age of the pies served at the finish, it is the race that everyone wants to do - so enter early! Karrimor Ltd, Petre Road, Clayton-le-Moors, Accrington, Lancs BB5 5JP.
MID NOVEMBER	THE COPELAND CHASE. In the Lakes. 10 & 15 miles 26 Culgarth Ave, Cockermouth, Cumbria CA13 9PL

There are hundreds of other fell races which only require navigation skills if the weather is bad. For details of these, see the Fell Runners Association Fixtures Booklet. The FRA can be contacted at; Pete Bland Sports, 34A Kirkland, Kendal, Cumbria, (0539) 731012.